13/80

Poems of the Past

A Collection of Poetry
2006-2014

Poems of the Past

For the Staff at
St. Peter's School,
Chelmsford, Essex.

But **especially** for **Karen P.**

With love & thanks.

And as always, for my family:
Lisa, Ed and Laura.

For permission requests, for other information or to just have an electronic 'chat', please write to me at

arcmwriting@gmail.com

To visit my website, please go to:

http://arcmwriting.weebly.com

Created and Printed in the United Kingdom.

ISBN 978-0-9931494-0-5

This is a **First Edition** in this format (will there EVER be a second…).

CONTENTS

PREFACE

I was moved to write a poem for my daughters' very first teacher (yes she is that good) and then tried to 'place' it in the canon of what I hubristically call my poetry. And as I was idly leafing through the poems of the recent past to see if any (at all) had merit; I began wondering if, finally, I should do anything with them.

To me, your first teacher is important. *(No, **really** important)*. They can infuse you with a fervour to learn that can stay with you for many years, or fail to spark in you the enjoyment of learning that can make school a little bit more difficult in years to come.

My daughter's first teacher Karen (See both St. Peter's Teachers and A Note for Teacher) is lovely. A thoughtful professional with a wicked sense of humour. [In fact, all of the Teachers, the Head and indeed the whole Staff and Pupil body at the school seem to be the sort of people that my lovely girl needs around her to start her education off in the best way possible].

They are not perfect, and nor as parents can we expect them to be; but they really do their best. I plucked up the courage and, feeling very brave (she is a TEACHER after all!) I gave the poem I had written to her.

And then, at the end of the summer term, before Laura moved onto a new class and a new teacher, Karen said:

"I'd like a signed copy of your anthology when it's published".

Now, to someone so wrapped up in themselves that they write poetry about things around (and inside of) them; this really fired a thought process. I already had two other collections nearing (self) publication, had dug out some older poetry collections and short stories written many years ago; so I thought, why not look at producing a third collection – this time of more recent poems not specifically about any one subject?

Now I wish I could say that I'm one of those people who consider that if something is not good enough, it should be destroyed. I wish I could say that, but in all honesty, I cannot. If I did that, I'd have nothing. I keep everything - snippets, phrases, elements; parts of lines – anything and everything that I write or overhear. If I have not finished it at the time of writing; I keep it, usually never using it again.

I write, I save and I archive just about everything (part of an OCD issue I think). Almost all of the poems I write arrive on the page (or usually the screen) fully formed and requiring only a little polish to 'complete' them (as if I ever can). I think of a phrase, a line or the 'beat' of a sound and the poem starts to whirl in my mind and take shape, even as I turn on my phone and access the Notes app, or scrabble for a pen and pad.

Archiving and keeping everything becomes a little difficult sometimes, as I always like to give someone a version of a poem written for them that is unique. Thus, if the poem is *for* someone (and I had the courage to give it to them) then there are at least two copies in existence; my 'adjusted' copy and **their** totally original version. Even if (as is most of the time) what I produce on the page is not what I 'saw' in my head (and thus not good enough); I keep it. In truth, usually just to try to achieve something closer to what I see in my mind when the poem starts to rise in my mind.

Not all of the poetic (or lyrical) output written by me during these years has been included here. If you are a 'completionist' (as I am); then there are other collections for you to find. Two of these are in the 'Sleeping' strand of work. This series started with 'Silent as Sleeping' (for my Father) and more recently 'Another One Sleeping' (for my Mother) after their deaths. The subject matter involved is obviously not 'light', but it does cover a lot of themes, including the births of both my Son and Daughter, and life after. Although there will be more historical (and I hope future) collections in due course; these three are the only one's currently released into the wild.

This collection is of the 'recent' past; from the only one I seem to have written in 2006, across the years to the many more written in 2013 and (up to November) in 2014. None of them are perfect, none of them can be (just look who wrote them); but I think that at least a few have some worth, some phrase or element that could resonate with someone, maybe you.

But if that is *not* you, then I apologise and do not expect you to stay. If, however, you see something, feel something or hear something that you like; then sit down, rest, pause a moment and dive in. I hope you will feel it time pleasantly spent.

As a final word, I think it worth suggesting here that, if possible, you consider reading these poems aloud to yourself. Poetry, intricate delicacies on small spoons; can be savoured via the voice of the mind, and much is too good effect. But I believe that the music in poetry (if there is any in mine and I hope that there is) is best discovered, best experienced with the aural participation of the 'reader'. By reading the poem aloud (where possible without eliciting the stares and interventions of others), you may hear the metre, the pattern, the *music* that is in the poem and thus experience it in a different way; and that might prove more pleasurable.

However you choose to experience these offerings of mine, indeed whether you do or do not, I wish you the best and hope that, if you do not receive that you want, you at least receive what you need.

Alan R C Mitchell
Chelmsford, Essex
November 2014

A Photo of the author

Poems of the Past

FEAST

I feast on failure – and full am I –
fit for futures as yet unseen;
I hide behind mirrors - as glass reflects you -
deflects the things they might have seen.

All smoke and mirrors, insubstantial form
The laughs disrupt enquiring minds;
but some see through this, some pinpoint me
amazed -or not- at what they find.

Some feast on futures, gorge on promise
yet just like shadows, I hide within;
and write these darkling's, vent my anger
waiting 'til my life begins.

You sit so quiet, tall yet troubled
cocooned in strength you meet them all
and they mistake you, not see truth there,
waiting for the mask to fall?

Akin in spirit? Wishful think I
Success you've had, success I lack
- this is not moaning, nor whingeing really
perhaps should try another tack -

I feast on failure, you look at promise
The flipside of one basic thought;
That to those people who spin around us
Never are we truly caught.

For Roger Whale
21st February 2006

LONDON DIARY

Pretty girls with perfect teeth
Glimpsed so quickly and then move on
Makeup matters, see the girl there
In the carriage she puts it on.

Trips to London, work to do
You groan with pain and lift your bag
Walking slowly, far to go now
You reach the stairs and start to sag

The life of London, pass it on;
Is nothing new but very old.
The sounds of London; pass them on
Are something special growing old.

Sit on train or stand on tube
Are pressed against the newly washed
Avoiding eyes with hands in pockets
Because you are so neatly squashed.

You smell the hair, you see it shining
Wonder how long she was in the bath.
A girl gets on, pushing fiercely
You catch an eye and share a laugh

The life of London, pass it on;
Is nothing new but very old.
The sounds of London; pass them on
Are something special, growing old.

A thousand faces seen in minutes
They pass in front of puzzled eyes.
And all those people, eyes ablaze
Will never wonder at my surprise.

That they don't know the world around them
And never know the thrill of me.
They bustle past, looking downwards,
avoiding eyes so as not to see.

The life of London, pass it on;
Is nothing new but very old.
The sounds of London -pass them on-
Are something special, growing old

3rd December 2008

INTO A WORLD OF THREE, COMES ONE

The news surprised me, scared me so
It changed my world, my life, my time.
So unexpected, yet so exciting
I knew that it would change my mind.

Will it be boy or girl for us?
A daughter or a newer son?
All I know, now forever
Into a world of three, comes one

Of all three lives here, getting on,
Making here a life for three.
But now there's four and I am frightened
Love and pressure I can see

Will it be boy or girl for us?
A daughter or another son?
All I know, now forever
Into a world of three, comes one.

I work so hard, and ask so little
A decaff coffee and time to be
And now it changes, and gladly will I
Lift my eyes and then to see

Will it be boy or girl for us?
A daughter or another son?
All I know, now forever
Into a world of three, comes one

She is so tired, it's all a battle
I do my best but fear I fail.
And when she gets upset or tearful,
I hold her close and tell the tale

Of these three people, living together
Side by side they soldier on.
And then from nowhere, one more joins them
Into a world of three, comes one.

For Lisa
3rd December 2008

ANOTHER BORN

And so another; and just like Brian
You stop a moment and a friend has gone.
This is the cycle, moving onwards,
Is so unreal when put in song.

This man (remember, smiling always?)
Caught your eye you made a friend.
But Terry died then, leaving family
You never had a chance to send

Your thanks for knowing
Your hopes of growing
The times you spent
The laughs you shared.

I did not know him, not like others,
Not like Brian in truth to tell
But I did like him and mourn his passing
Mourn another who too quickly fell.

And I just sit here, shocked and angry,
I never got to say goodbye
I didn't know the pain of parting
I didn't know the day he died.

Your thanks for knowing
Your hopes of growing
The times you spent
The laughs you shared.

Is not important, is not required,
This is not here 'bout you and me.
If I can stop you, slow you shortly
Raise your eyes and heart to see

That here immortal, friend for lifetime
In my mind he'll always stay.
As life is ending, as people mourn him
Another's born to greet the day

Another's born to greet the day
Another's born to greet the day

For Terry
26th January 2009

EMPTY HOUSES

Flowers hang like gifts to God
that undetected fade away.
Faces pass like deep in fog
Quickly gone by end of day.

People sit and read and sleep
Passing lives that pass away
The train that rumbles; safe to keep
Our secrets silent and not to say

That we remember all the signs
That tumbled slowly to the ground
And laughed and played our days away
And never sold the friends we found.

In a world of music chosen
From so much I like to hear.
I pass the journey, almost frozen
By internal major fear.
Passing billboards, saying nothing
Reading lines in others' eyes
Watching houses, passing, leaving
Remembering with such surprise

That we remember all the signs
That tumbled slowly to the ground
And laughed and played our days away
And never sold the friends we found.

Thus into station, one phase done now
Will I have the strength I need
To give the words I wrote for them now
To help them go where others lead.

That we remember all the signs
That tumbled slowly to the ground
And laughed and played our days away
And never sold the friends we found.

Pass couples kissing with eyes so closed
They could not see the brightest light.
We leave behind now, weeping gently
We pass through lives and out of sight.
And now the final stage of journey
Move towards the end of day.
Attend the funeral, smile for memory
And live our lives and come what may.

Also For Terry
26th January 2009

IT IS THERE

All these people living softly,
Like a poet in the rain
All the time this music's playing,
I can't escape the sad refrain

All the glittering of prizes,
Stacked up high among the heights
And you stand within this tower,
Watch an ocean full of lights.

See the myriad of people
Walk the myriad of miles
Is there spirit in their voices
Is there laughter in their smile?

As we fly over the canyon,
See the majesty nature made
I can see the depth of water,
Let us hope it never fades

Back in town we take a bus ride,
On the top deck, see it all
As the lights of town pass by us,
Pass a Chapel that's so small

See the myriad of people
Walk the myriad of miles
Is there spirit in their voices
Is there laughter in their smile?

Walking through the biggest hotel,
That I've ever been inside
is a room so large, a cavern,
That you swim, a shoal, a tide

All the noise, the smoke, the people,
All the trappings of a life
Never kept but always gambled,
With the Lady Luck of Life

See the myriad of people
Walk the myriad of miles
Is there spirit in their voices
Is there laughter in their smile?

So we move, another City,
For a day we take a tour
Through this city full of Angels,
through this money that's a lure

Now back home I find I miss it,
Find I pine for buildings tall
When I sleep it's there I'm dreaming,
And I hear that country call.

Through the poetry of motion
Through the artistry of sound
It is there in truth I'm living
It is there in truth I'm bound.

1959
28th October 2012

DEFEATED

Defeated I feel, adrift from my life
though I have two great children
a house and a wife

Defeated by life, ground down by it all
and hearing so clearly
another life call

I'll walk into Sunset; I'll walk into years
I'll leave behind daydreams –
And all of my fears

Adrift from connections that enhance your days
I shelter behind them and count out the ways
That I've not been honest or truthful or right
Or hidden in darkness and away from the light

I'll walk into sunset, I'll walk into years
I'll leave behind daydreams –
And all of my fears

I deal in the painting of words in your mind
But fail to achieve it, in what will I find
The rest that I crave, the peace that I seek
Beyond just the pause at the end of the week

I'll walk into sunset, I'll walk into years
I'll leave behind daydreams –
And some of my tears

New countries to visit and New voices to hear
Within all this darkness the path is not clear
And I will not leave them, my children, for fear
That they will not need me
I'll fade from their view
And all I'll be left with
Are pictures of you

I'll walk into sunset, I'll walk into years
I'll leave behind daydreams - And some of my tears

1539
7th November 2012

RIVEN

I never meant to hurt you
I never meant to cause you pain
I only wanted answers
To change the meaning of my name

You never seem to see me
you never seem to need me here
You never seem to want me
I never meant to bring you tears

There is a truth in all this
There is a truth that you won't see
A complex situation
And lives are changing, all at sea

The angers always there now
our baggage heavy, too hard to bear
Frustration is the norm here
for all the fact we used to care

These angered situations
this shattering of life and past
May end our time together
a future riven from the past

I need my children's faces,
I need to hear their voices call
whatever else that happens
They are my future
They are my all.

Is this why no-one likes me?
My sense of loss for all to see
A damaged piece of flotsam
Alone, adrift upon the sea

I wanted understanding
To find out why a baby died
I needed resolution
To find out why she didn't lie

I am not guilty of this
I did not do the things you say
But I'll be here forever
To see my children
Come what may.

So talk or not, I cannot
Change the way you look at me
And maybe I don't want too
Perhaps in anger you will see

That we are wrong, a burden
We have to change, apart or not
To carry on in this way
Is not the only choice we've got

So I will stay and love them
They are my children, I love them all
And you and I don't matter
It is for them I'd give my all.

0958
29th November 2012

I WILL NOT

I will not bend or break from this
I will not heal or mend
I will not cry myself to sleep
Or just my spirit send

I'll just hold on as in my heart
I know the truth of all
And though this hurts and pains me so
And like a lion maul

I'll stay right here for good or ill
I'll stay for childhood's sake
And though it rips and tears at me
The best of this I'll make

Love holds hands no more with me
It left me like a stone
The need for deed and loving arms
Was merely mine, alone

Although I've failed I did my best
Was all that I could be
And in the end what else is there?
What else is there to see?

I'll stay right here for good or ill
I'll stay for childhood's sake
And though it rips and tears at me
The best of this I'll make

0958
29th November 2012

WE STAND

We stand stock still in serried ranks,
Those off to work those off to banks
Inside a silent stately hall
Where no-one hears another's call
But wait for bus to come along
So we can board and "move along!"
So we can sit in quiet faith
The god of work (that special race)
And leave again our homes behind
To look for truth we seldom find
We number many yet no-one speaks
For fear of being labelled freaks
We stand as islands alone at sea
We let them settle, we let them be.

Bus 0812
17th March 2013

WE SIT

We sit like sheep within their pens
like cattle lowing or noisy hens
On train to Town for work are we
we sleep by windows so we can't see
The journey through this land of ours
We pass them walking or in their cars
But trapped inside our lonely minds
We speak to no-one, "*don't cross the line*!"
That separates the known from not
be happy with the lot you've got
Check the diary of things to do
and where to be and to be who?
For on this journey to town today
you could be happy, in your way.

Train 0840
17th March 2013

WE WALK

We walk the station, to catch a train
To let the DLR take strain
And move us mainly to somewhere else
Where we can find a hint of self
A mass of many, a shepherd proud
For we are not in talking loud
But feet that march these hallowed halls
Are watched by people's past foot-falls
And when we sneeze, or yawn or cough
No human contact; it's not enough
To say so quiet 'excuse me please'
For few acknowledge the subtle sneeze
To be together, to share this train
To share life's journey should be the aim.

DLR 0920
17th March 2013

A BETTER FATHER

I'm a better father than I am a man
I'm a better brother than I am a man
It's not hard to see the way of things
When you see in the mirror the meaning life brings

So a better husband is what I want in life
But for that to work - a better wife
It's not hard to see in the darkness of night
The turning of angels to see perfect light

0841
17th June 2013

TURNING FOREVER

Turning forever, our time marches on
the planets surround you, it won't be for long
you look up and smile, it will take a while
To reach out to you.

Perfect conduction, we spark and we glow
And the people who see you that are in the know,
You look up and smile, it will take a while
To reach out to you.

We turn forever in the sky
we make decisions and comply
we turn forever in the sky
we look to heaven and then sigh

Outside production, inside the dream
we buy all the paintings including the scream
you look up and smile, it will take a while
to reach out to you.

Reviewing decisions, reviewing the plan
we stand all so closely mould into a man
you look up and smile, it will take a while,
to reach out to you.

We turn forever in the sky
we make decisions and then cry
we turn forever in the sky
we look to heaven and comply

2225
28th August 2013

WHAT WILL BE LEFT?

What will be left when I'm no longer here?
What will I leave -
             'cept this small drying tear?

We live and love and laugh and cry
and seldom seek to ask the why
Running headlong to oblivion in the faces that we
see
Try to find a fit solution for all of us to be

And I sit and I wonder what will there then be
Of this large framed cathedral and the spirit that is
me
My son wouldn't miss me; is not aware that I'm
alive
While my daughter is so lovely, will continue now
to thrive

A few lines of verse no one bothers to read
as it's written to counter this deep inner need
so it's selfish, as I am in so many a way
but I know that I'll always want,
yet another full day.

1347
28th August 2013

A LIFE HALF OVER

A life half over, a life half bought,
a man half living and without a thought.
The day's past caring, the day's long gone,
The man left wishing that he could belong

The stress is pressure, the pressure is clear
You have to do it, overcome all your fear
The song is so subtle, the song is so loud
You have to make everyone here so proud

But time is running, and running free
How to slow it, to become the 'me'
The man past standing and mindful of life
As he watches his family, his children and wife
Become more than they could be, as they take to
the wing
Leave him behind them as they learn how to sing

A life half over, a life half thought
A man barely living in this life he has caught
The day more than over, the darkness is near
If only his pathway for rest was as clear.

1015
13th September 2013

SECRET

What do you see when you look in my eyes
Can you see that I mean what I say?
That I didn't do the thing that you said
that I really didn't mean it that way

You see me and know me, the things that I do
for after all you are my wife
it's a shame that you hate this part of my world
this other side of my life

It causes us anger, resentment and pain
for both of us have to then hide
I wish we could find a suitable choice
a way to soon swim with the tide

We should try all we can to find such a way
to find a way through this sad mess
I would like it a lot, for the sake of myself
if just once in a while you would say 'yes'

I know that you're stressed, afraid and concerned
at the changes to work and to life
but I love you so much and I want you to be
a more rounded part of my life.

1147
21st November 2013

I HAVE A FRIEND

I have a friend - perhaps that's too strong a word -
for I knew him years ago

An egocentric - yet lovely man (at least he was back
then) -
we lost touch so long ago

And then I found - these social media sites you
know -
His world again and watched it pass once more

From outside in - it's easy to lurk and watch the
words scroll by -
It looked (as always), he'd kept the perfect life

Was happy but unsurprised - blessed he was in
form and format -
I'd always lost when compared to him

I watched his travels - honestly he trips the world
with ease -
As I stayed home and cared for those so young

He seemed so settled - acting life in front and on a
wider stage -
I envied him his easy life, and access to the sun

And then an update - on sites you do, if not each
day, at least each week -
It caught my eye as inner glimpse did make

"The cancer's gone" - he said quite quiet and made me start -
Was thrown away, that line

But made me stop - and realise really quite late in life -
That all can seem fine, from a distance.

16th December 2013

BENT & BROKEN

Umbrellas stand and sit all broken,
Bent like owners clothes now soaken
Rushing through the gushing stain
Without a cover to stave off rain
That pours and creeps like inner rage
And spoils the ink on printed page
As over heads they push their paper
Covering now but can't use later
Umbrellas dead and lie like road kill
Twisted, black they lie there until
Picked by cleaners with covered heads
To far away to hear what's said
And in this city, with all its stories
Each dead one hints at long gone glories.

City of London
11th Feb 2014

LIST

Ever think about your funeral music?
(I do. I do)
Love Theme from 'Blade Runner'
As the coffin arrives
And the people all stand around
with their reddening eyes.

'Could've told you before I met You'
At the interlude for thoughts
Or 'Resin on my Heart strings'
As my life comes down to naught

Or 'Fading Lights' to capture
soft the feelings of the day
Or one I've written, or a poem perhaps
to show my own special way

There are so many songs and sounds
that might connect with how I feel
yet what, at end, do I want to say
what do I want to make real?

This List refines and changes yes
As moods and hopes portends
My main regret, I will not see
The few who may attend.

Stratford
13th Feb 2014

DLR

People stand, or sit and watch
The trains pass by them, faces flashing
The tunnels rush and eat us whole
And spit us out to water rushing

The whole world's cold and lonely right now
Layered with the grime of ages
All who travel heed no other
Cast down eyes to turn the pages

Blue sky comes but just for moments
as clouds once more foretell the downfall
of light and warmth, the people huddle
waiting for life to start again, that's all

DLR
13th February 2014

THE DEAD AND DYING

The dead and dying scenes of night
that grant your dreams a darker light
are mixed with faces old and new
not many left now, there are too few

You left behind or were left yourself
A once-used toy unloved on shelf
You grip so tightly past glories few
And bluster and ignore that there are no new

But on you go, another day
to pass or fail in your own way
you wake too early, sleep too light
dream those dreams that scare you right

To core, the centre of what you are
all on a journey to go so far
yet who will finish the race yet run
and wake to greet tomorrow's sun?

Stratford DLR
13th February 2014

MARRIAGE

So Donna you will marry
and give yourself new name
Embark once more upon a path
And nothing will be the same

You've had a varied and turbulent time
But made the best through all
and now, at last, have heard the voice
of love's most strongest call

Am happy that you start afresh
and stand in church so dressed.
And shine with pride and beauty that
Not many would have guessed

The sadness, pain and difficulties
you've overcome, endured.
And now with man to love you so
Your life can be assured

So into world of marriage again
and into world you go.
Remember all those years since gone
I really did tell you so!

24th February 2014

FEATURE
FAILURE
FAST &
FLAG

Feature, failure, fast and flag
the loss of honour will make you sad
the lack of pain would be such a boon
the hope is that it could start sometime soon

Conflict, cannon cause and crash
to feel the bite of the bully's lash
to be so bereft and sad and in pain
and know from their eyes that it won't be the same

Portrait, pistol pride and pause
to escape the chance to give them cause
to show the truth, the right, the strength
of service given over such a length

Friction fireworks flex and fool
to get to the end is the general rule
to support my family for all that I'm worth
for as long as my days last here on this earth.

5th April 2014

FINALLY FALL

A friend whose father has fallen like mine
Bereft and now beaten, and run out of time
Am left here to wonder the way to reach out
And offer some comfort although that's in doubt

If could but now stretch out and touch with my
hand
The fingers of fathers now lost to this land
And save us from pain and the feelings of loss
Show him the care and what it has cost

Tell him that love does not dry like the rain
Feelings will linger yet not now the same
you lose who you love and can never then find
the faces in crowds, it's as if you are blind

Loving and losing and the knowledge of both
Is better than never having either so close
You treasure the time you have left with them all
Until you must answer and finally fall

It was good that I met him, but I care more for you
And would be there to answer, to soothe or to do
the little that can as it's never enough
it's the letting them go that is so very tough.

Home 2321
26th April 2014

THAT I

I heard from my son 'bout my friends fathers' death
and it all rushes inwards, the catching of breath
I would send him a message and tell him that I
would be there as a shoulder upon which to cry

I would tell him that I am now thinking of him
And that now it must start as a new phase begins
And how it will change him and the family whole
As it courses all through them and down to the soul

But I cannot and must not now pour out these thoughts
For its not here my help nor my counsel he sought
He has others to help and support him I'm hope
So I'll call in the morning and trust him to cope

That I feel so distressed at my friends sudden loss
That I know how it felt for my own world, the toss
Of a coin decides fates and the anger of man
At the helplessness feelings, you do what you can.

Home 2333
26th April 2014

GO GENTLE

Go gentle old man on the pathway you tread
With whisky in one hand and recently fed
Leave your cares and your pains and your children
behind
And let others now search for the truth that they
find
You leave us your children who will do you proud
As you float through the trees and the puffy white
clouds
You leave us your grand kids and soon even more
As a great grandchild moves down from a cloudy
upper floor
These words will mean nothing and may never be
read
In the writing, in the thinking, even if they're not
said
They are written for you and your family sad
I know you'll be missed and the times that were had
The dad's dinners change and may never repeat
For there'll be a chair there and empty
No one sits in that seat.

Home 2345
26th April 2014

WEEKEND FATHERS

These weekend-only fathers who all seem to be
Alive at the weekend when they may then see
the daughter or son who they love all they can
- but part-time and Sundays was not part of the
plan

The hugs and the kisses, the holding of hands
The need to possess them as long as they can
The subtle (quiet) question of what mum's up to
today
As they sit and watch them go off now to play

The hurt and the pain I can see in these eyes
Will not come as a shock or a similar surprise
These weekend-only fathers do the best that they
can
And rise over the failure that it is to be a man

McDonald's Boreham 1035
11th May 2014

NUMBERS

Is this all that's left at the end of a life
The loss of a husband and no longer a wife
The empty small house with no carpets or stairs
The memories of Mum in that old scrappy chair

The house has been sold, it completed today
the money's been banked yet what can I say
I'd rather have Mum than the money it's true
I feel list and lonely and from my point of view

The numbers are merely reflecting her worth
Best of the rest and the salt of the earth
I miss her and mourn her and thank her today
my sadness reflecting her own special way.

Home
16th May 2014

St. PETER'S TEACHERS

Hundreds of photos and thousands of faces
All in their ranks and all in their places
Down through the years and up through the classes
Changing their clothes but keeping their glasses

Children who smile and those that just stare
Teachers who stand and who radiate care
the sum of a school is more than its parts
this so special school is where it all starts

The children who sit through assembly time
Listening to others and singing the rhymes
the teachers who prompt, who advise and who
guide
praising the children that win and who tried

Sports days for all as we look to the skies
Fingers all crossed it's the sun that will rise
these people, these teachers, assistants and cooks
Caretakers, helpers who sit to read books

They shape all our children and help parents too
and special 'mid many, they are all too few.

Home
23rd May 2014

SETTLED

The dust has now settled, the mother returns
the work has resumed and the world will now turn
the way that you feel, as a family, and alone
is private, unvoiced, it is like you're a stone

I've not been in touch for a week now or more
I know that the feelings are still far too raw
I know that you stand, and you keep moving on
try to be strong and the best you can son

But I've thought of you often, both you and the rest
as you face all together this most family test
the fading of someone from your everyday lives
yet not gone is he and you will always now strive

to remember his voice, and his face and his smile
and the way that he looked in a room for a while
a father, a parent, a son in his way
you both face together, these feelings your way.

Home 1417
28th May 2014

I MISS HER

I miss her, I miss her, that soft little girl
Who smiles are like sunshine as she traces and curls
And the shape of her neck or her so perfect eyes
That look in such wonder as she soothes all my sighs
She is safe and with grandma who loves her as well
Yet I miss her I miss her and want now to tell
That the cuddles of morning or the warm hugs at night
Are the only thing shedding some perfect bright light
She's so fragile and joyful and her voice holds my mind
My heart is a sailboat that can sail when I find
She is here with me softly and strokes my old hand
And I hear all too loudly the rushing of sand

Home 1435
28th May 2014

CODEBREAKERS

My thoughtful response to the sadness inside
is you never can truly, your feelings here hide
they chase you, and rob you, and spin you to ground
laughing they race off at what they have found

to wound you as sun may now turn into rain
you wake up quite happy until hits you, the pain
you cry and you smile and you carry the day
forwards in time to face come what may

yet who sees inside the truth of a man?
you do what are able, and fail when you can
I hope you'll not mind this breaking of code
this stepping 'cross boundaries, an untaken road

I reach out with warmth and a quizzical smile
to touch you and tell you there are many miles
for you left here to travel, a journeying time
am here, in my spirit I share in this rhyme

I hope these will find you and perhaps let you see
you're held in the hearts of the friends that you see
we cannot now share in this grief that you hide
but through this, unspoken, we are on your side.

Home 1445
28th May 2014

ONE MORE MOMENT

One more moment is all that we ask
that breathing slow or breathing fast
we see once more the ones we lost
and count them all and count the cost
to hold their hand and fingers touch
to look in eyes of wonder

      such

        as in a child when sees the sun
And learns to walk and learns to run
And given back that fearful dread
What lies beyond is where we're led
So follow on or follow not
Tie yourself impossible knot
You cannot see or hear again
The gentle tapping of falling rain

You cannot now behold the eyes
yet sit in silent tearful
            Sighs

Home
3rd June 2014

FATHER'S DAY

Father's Day future and father's day past
Fathers are precious but not meant to last
we share all we can yet we lose so much more
we can't know the final time they'll walk out that
door

We love in a way that's not really real
and seldom do we say the things that we feel
a Father, a husband and once was a son
I sit and I think 'til this long day is done

So Father's day future and father's day past
and Fathers unborn will then soon face the task
we love them and love all the days we can find
as a Father, as a husband as a son (in my mind)

Home
15th June 2014

SEAGULLS

The sound of seagulls screaming
'cross the sunlit streets
In search of sky in search of love,
in search of things to eat
The beat of wings, the scream of voice so high,
ascending task
They swoop and turn and call above, their never
ending ask

I walk below, I walk so slow
an ageing man now lost
I see them high and yearn to fly
but cannot pay the cost
The seagulls call and mock my life (so high above
the street)
I hear them call and fly and fall and stand so still
to weep.

Chelmsford
24th June 2014

GIFTS

Gifts are showered (and some are flowers)
And some are chocolates too
The presents mean (just as it seems)
That everyone values you.

You touch our hearts (this varied cast)
And make a difference too
Your special eyes (and varied smiles)
Is what for us makes you.

So gifts are given, **and lies forgiven**
and all comes back to you
We try to be the best we can be
As really we just love you.

Home
29th June 2014

A NOTE FOR TEACHER

You've taught our girl, you've taught her well
How to write and how to spell
the various marks and different grades
the choices and decisions made

You've helped our daughter plus hundreds more
you've kept her safe and made her sure
and we give thanks now she moves up
we raise a glass or raise a cup

And thank you Karen for all you've done
for what you've meant and now begun
she'll move on through the system now
to become what we know not how

And in your class she learnt to try
to 'give it a go' and try to fly
the journey starts, the step is made
the memories of you will never fade.

Another class, another trace
to fix the game and run the race
we'll miss your style, your wit and grace
You taught us well Miss, we'll miss your face.

Train
24th June 2014

For Laura's First Teacher.
Just because you're KP doesn't mean that you're nuts...

BIRTHDAY GREETINGS

Birthday greetings sent from places
that I haven't long time seen

Letters online sending wishes
from the faces not long seen

One is missing, writing long gone,
miss the sight of written name

Mother, Father now no longer,
life can never be the same

But thank you all, wife and family,
friends of mine who stand by me

I welcome wishes,
thoughts and cards now,

I look towards what now
Might Be.

Home
7th July 2014

GOSSAMER

Gossamer webs like cradles cuddling
Trail across the browning grass
Misty mornings, sunrise hidden
Moon is waning, fading fast

Sun breaks through, reveals the water
covering green oceans ground
Webs of water glint and shatter
Glasslike fronds are what I found

Air heats up and moisture moving
Swirling through the heavy air
I turn around and breathe in deeply
at nature's bounty I merely stare

Home 0914
16th July 2014

WE REST A WHILE

Friends now scattering for the summer
as school days end
We rest a while
We'll see so few now for over six weeks
while holidays happen
We rest a while

The tears for leavers, the new ones coming
the school moves on
like Seasons do.
The joy and laughter and quiet sadness
the still reflection by just a few

We rest a while at coloured school gates
we rest a while and think of you
each schoolchild carries into future
the hopes of many, the dreams of few.

So friends now scatter across this small globe,
they venture out
We rest a while
This isolation among the sunshine
the school moves on
We rest a while

Home 0928
16th July 2014

HOSPITAL GOWN

How many people have worn this before?
Thrown over a chair or kicked round the floor
Washed and cleaned to the utmost degree
Packed and presented as if just for me

The cloth not so thin that it's see-through in places
but washed and so faded I can see all their faces:
the nurses and care staff who've given it out
to men, maybe women, for their rear ends to flout

It ties up in knots at the back and the neck
Is short and immodest and so very low tech
Yet it does it, the job it's designed here to do
To signal to all that you're no longer you.

Broomfield Hospital 1715
29th July 2014

HOW MANY

How many moments like these
that sit on wing or ride on breeze
That flaunt to air and cry and sing
and like around you bells will ring
Before the daily end will bring?

Home 0008
5th August 2014

CAR WASH

His eyes in back of car as started
Tears to fall as rain was parted
Washing car before its sale
Yet made him cry this noise, and wail

I close my own and see his fear
so young in day, in month, in year
In back of car to wash all clean
yet only was his terror seen

I held out hand and watched them fall
from red eyes round the tears would call
my mem'ry back across the years
to see my young boy's sudden fears.

Home 0014
5th August 2014

RIP

The man with those eyes and the fistful of voices
Looked in his mind through a myriad of choices
sat in his house on the warmest of coasts
With money, success, the most genial of hosts

The outward mask that he wore every day
the funniest lines that his lips would then say
Belied a sad man who could not handle tears
Who desired an ending for his own inner fears

So he left us with memories and his sharp witty
faces
and we mourn him and miss him from the funniest
of places
and wish to have been, if only we could!
An ear for to turn too at the end would have stood

In his way for a moment and asked him to pause
And to ask him if ever we could give him a cause
That would keep him around in this world, in this
life
Would have held him and soothed him to let go of
the strife

But could not have and did not it could never have
been
For I watched him and laughed at his faces on
screen
As culpable I, as the rest that I saw
For enjoying, but not seeing, his own inner war

Home 2250
12th August 2014
For Robin Williams

TESTS

More doctors and more nurses
more blood taken, and soft curses
the pains in my body may never now go
the frightening outcome – I'll not even know
Dismissive of speaking, he sat back in his chair
hunched as a lion asleep in a lair
No answers, but tests and a long way to go
Return in two months
After that
Who may know?

Broomfield 1650
19th August 2014

SHARK FIN

Shark fin slice through cloudy haze
Coloured fins flash 'cross my gaze
circling, moving watching all
Waiting for the tannoy call

Sea so vast they cross like flies
Lumbering into cloudy skies
Taxi queue of silver tubes
People crammed in seats so few

Shark fins slice and cut and fly
People wait and talk, so dry
the tension builds and pause until
the scream of engines ears will fill

And in the shark, that tube, that fin
we fit ourselves so deep within
And fly to coast so far away
Yet leave behind a son today.

Gatwick Gate 50 1544
27th August 2014

TAKE OFF

holding hands and gripping finger
tension in the air that lingers
Shouts and cries as thunder sound
fills the air, we leave the ground

now into air the gases streaming
over engines full and screaming
up to clouds, to burst through air
for us the grounds' now no longer there

I look to wife whose eyes are crying
look to daughter, small and smiling
look through plastic Perspex crazing
with the earth below
Amazing

Runway 737-800 1650
27th August 2014

AIRBORNE

The bumpy air, the mottled smells
Inside bottles' a special hell
the pings of asking fliers few
the too small seats that restrain you

The noisy snorers asleep so soon
the jostling kids still seeking room
the headphones on, the Kindle readers
The Magazine and TV teasers

All fly through updrafts, steady air
without the ground, without a care
we travel on, we fly through space
we leave our lives, we leave the race.

36000' 1714
27th August 2014

FRAGILE DAYS

A friend of mine, his father died
I do not know who was by side
I never met nor spoke to him
nor knew his name (was not his kin)

I spoke of him to friend of mine
when my Mum died, and at that time
He knew his dad could not get through
This saddest time that comes to you

That comes to all upon this rock
a quick release or sudden shock
an ending in so many ways
beginning too, to count the days

These fragile days of mixtured thoughts
of what life is, and what it ought
To be for all at our final time
I fail to show in these few lines.

Chelmsford 1655
11th September 2014

For Tony Barnes and his Family

MARCHING

Time marches on, it hurts me so
it marches fast and marches slow
we move through space, through lives, through
time
we pick our way across the line

It marches now, we leave behind
the lives of others we cannot find
it marches on (I grieve you know)
for Mum and Dad, now in the flow

it marches fast, the faces fade
The mem'ry lapses, the hidden glade
I miss them all, I miss them now
I know not when, I know not how

But 'midst the time that marches on
and all the loved ones now long gone
I'll see again in heaven's heart
and turn to face a lifetime start

Home 1855
6th October 2014

ANOTHER GONE

Another gone to fly above
to soar with kestrels and with doves
to seek new place away from life
leaving children, left a wife
no reasons known for him to go
it is not right that I should know
not knew him well – not spoke for years
I keep inside my own, few tears
Yet know his family, bereft will be
and at this time cannot now see
the why's and wherefores that he should go
away from here and into flow
of time away, above, and fly
to distant sunshine, new life to try

Home 0845
7th October 2014

For Andy P and his Family

THE RAIN

The rain on the windows, the patterns of sound
the warmth of a duvet as if underground
the mild mannered darkness, the filtering light
the top of a head stowed way out of sight

returns me to youth and an earlier time
my lying in bed with my idling rhymes
my Mum in the kitchen, the twin tub aglow
and warm fuzzy smells to my bedroom would flow

the smell of the washday, the sounds of the
housework
melting away with the rain on the paintwork
am back now to these strangely middle-aged years
confronting my youth with my old aged fears

reviewing the memories, the loss and the gain
we all play our part in this catastrophic game
but I see her in kitchen, see him near the wall
and wait once again for my name, them to call

Home 1855
6th October 2014

A NEW ADDITION

A new addition arrived today,
our world is brighter in this small way
the friends and family who'll dote and coo
the Facebook buddies who'll watch and view

a little dot, a little girl
those little eyes and fingers curled
Two loving parents who'll fuss and bond
A little girl that goes beyond

the limits of love for all concerned
she'll grow up cute, all lives upturned
a glamorous granny, proud granddad too
waiting to love the three of you

Waiting to dote, to smile and care
She's on her journey; the steps are there
A life before her, a changing world
Remember the moments in your hand she's curled

Home 1932
9th October 2014

For River, what song will you sing?

For AP

Kicking through the autumn leaves
the crisp cold wind on face
I think of how all people leave
some with skill, with grace

some with sadness, some so sad
their timing is their own
Yet all will know what's left behind
The tragic seeds are sown

With pen and words or on a screen
we mark these passing days
and say goodbye within ourselves
to someone's special ways

So goodbye friend, I did not know
the deepest grief you kept
I hope that now, you have some peace
forget those times you wept

Home 1240
22nd October 2014

For Andy

AUTUMN PARK

At park at last, it is too fast
the way this life must go
My girl by side and she will ride
The things the park will show
She talks to me and I can see
The woman she will become
In time, in truth beyond her youth
She'll be my little one.

The sun up high the bluest sky
An autumn day did see
I love this girl, this subtle whirl
It feels like she's for me
My son in North and striding forth
Each footfall takes away
My daughter here can always steer
My life extends a day

West Hanningfield Park 1435
27th October 2014

SILVER SHOES

The candles burning with a flame
that burns so soft yet lights again
the Bride who walks in silver shoes
to meet the Groom and never lose

The love eternal that lights their eyes
they found each other, such soft surprise
they chose each other, so soon entwined
to raise above all of our kind

For something past so long begun
a dress so right it came from Mum
The garter new and something blue
they found a love for each, so true

And we all stand to watch the walk
to hear the words, take in the talk
'Among these people here today...'
New life for you and come what may

 come for you all, you two (four more)
For at your hearts, yes at your core
there is this love we all can see
You start your journey and become free

Home 1445
11th November 2014

For Emma & Simon & family on your Wedding

WINTER

On the layered leaf meal mould
the setting sun will die
the crisp clean edge of breath will
softly, on the airflow lie

The keenest edge of winters knife
the darkness creeping in
the colours falling to the ground
as if a sign of sin

The school in shadow looming large
the offices alight
the glowing embers of the day
that sink into the night

The chilled harsh air that I breathe in
the memories I contain
will never visit here once more
can never come again

The prayers unanswered float to sky
as leaves fall to the ground
And all our dreams are captured here
They rise without a sound.

St. Peter's 1610
20th November 2014

SMUG

She walks so sweetly
   with marching arms
I smile and want to hug

  my gorgeous girl,
my sweet, my dream
   I feel a little smug

Riverside 1710
20th November 2014

LIFE RUNS RAGGED

My life runs ragged, and running slow
I sit and think of this
I see all now as if through fog
they all walk in a mist

My son afar and learning more
we thought he ever would
my daughter close, an early stage
and tries all that she should

My mind breaks down; I catch it swift
and run it through my mind
The piercing sounds of others near
alleged others of my kind

I try my best, I do the most
Yet fail, of that I'm sure
And in this time and in this place
I know there is no cure

Riverside 1729
20th November 2014

BLUE LIGHTS

Lights now flashing in the darkness
full of volume, noises ride
House lights shine but fail in fullness
moving people to the side

People mix and mingle slowly
lights that blink and volume loud
Youngsters walk and stumble sometimes
lost among the growing crowd

This is not a scene of failure
but party for a Lady here
Birthday Wishes, all for Jacky
voices raised to sing and cheer

Blue lights, green and other colours
Swirl amid the frenzied dance
Music loud and pulsing greatly
people miss the sudden glance

People sing, or dance, or missing
walk outside to get some air
Watch the doors from out the darkness
Happy Birthday – people care.

Romford RFC 2154
22nd November 2014

For Jacky D

SHE PLAYS ALONE

She plays alone, that soft little girl
now the roundabout is free
She tried to play, to spin and laugh
to join those other three.

She watches all and sings along
she joins the Frozen theme
She loves her dress, I love her so
(I hope these kids aren't mean)

Now not alone! Now with some girls
they spin and laugh so much
I watch so proud, with tear in eye
I love my kids so much

Maces Playce 1730
28th November 2014

BUBBLES

the bubbles float
          and turn and fly
      and spin in colours
            here
  the eyes of these
          enchanted girls
    brings now
a subtle tear

      my daughter waves
            and sings along
To Olaf, Elsa too
     the snow machine
         brings winter close
the bubbles
     all too few

             Maces Playce 1830
             28th November 2014

Index of First Lines

Index of First Lines

I hope you enjoyed some of these...

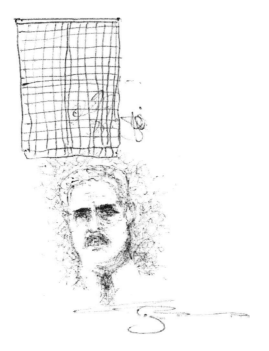

A sketch of the author
By artist Tony Barnes

Completed in a few minutes on the side of a
paper coffee cup (a Latte), London, January 2014.

Published by kind permission.

You can find more of Tony's artwork online at:

http://barnesart.weebly.com/

If you would like to find out more about the things I write, then please visit my website:

http://arcmwriting.weebly.com

Or to just get in touch, contact me via:

arcmwriting@gmail.com

Oh and you could always look out for more Poems and a Selection of collected Short Stories, coming in 2015!

I'd also like to thank Karen D at Grange House Publishing for her help, advice and patience!